IF WINTER COMES

Poems

Satyapal Anand

Order this book online at www.trafford.com
or email orders@trafford.com

Most Trafford titles are also available at major online book retailers.

Printed in the United States of America.

ISBN: 978-1-4669-1006-5 (sc)
ISBN: 978-1-4669-1007-2 (hc)
ISBN: 978-1-4669-1005-8 (e)

Library of Congress Control Number: 2011963604

Trafford rev. 01/03/2011

 www.trafford.com

North America & international
toll-free: 1 888 232 4444 (USA & Canada)
phone: 250 383 6864 ✦ fax: 812 355 4082

So thou hast come, O Winter

FOR

DAISY
&
SACHIN

Contents

Oedipus is sunk in thought

Whatever I've seen with these mortal eyes
When suddenly the eye lens break into smithereens
And in a shattered moment of time
Caste their spell over my past
What would I do?

Eyes, my silently loquacious Argus limb—
Only they will be eloquent like Psyche's
That caught love in its own wiles?
Wrapped in white and shuttered in the coffin
I've been counting moments turning into years
Lit by the promethean fire;
Is it a demon-dream they see each time they open?
The sparkling spell of self-hatred they cast over me
Will for centuries after I shut them
And hope to be a blind bat—unable to fly.

Would I ever be able to cry
Copious tears rolling my dead cheeks?
Have I no swollen creeks eager to break all dams?
No tears, no remorse, no self-cleansing, no nothing.
Even yet, Hamlet of yesteryears
A sordid tale of today
Lie in my coffin and with dead eyes
Hearse and rehearse the scenes I've seen
Much better if I had not witnessed them!

Eyes were the culprits
It were these Argus limbs that didn't go blind
When they perceived the truth

And had to be gotten rid of.
Guilt-ridden culpable eyes are out now
But my sinless memory of them
Has a million eyes—equally sly
Guileful and wicked.
The scenes they show me day and night
Impossible they are to watch again.

A million eye-apertures in my memory
How can I blind them? Oedipus is sunk in thought.

Body Prosody

I can only say that I knew nothing of its grammar.
Indeed—it is such a mixed up poetic text
My hands would put a noun before an adjective or
a double negative just for the sake of emphasis
Subject-verb inconsonance all the time
and, somehow I can still read the text and its meaning.
Understood it? Well, yes, in a way, not fully but, yes, in parts.

A poetic text for interpretation needs knowledge of prosody
but my hands, the topographers, were busy exploring all the time.
They never could differentiate between—what critics call—
the Syntax and layers in meaning, the Rhetoric and Speech.
When finger-tips feel multiple Accentual Syllables
scattered all over, Stress-patterns in Stanza.
Tetrameter, Pentameter, Hexameter were just words
translated into three, five or six—but how did they help
in my exploration? Indeed, they didn't.

An *iamb* is an accentual-syllabic verse, I had read
but (not as much my fingers as my lips) found an *iamb*
every next inch, a tetrameter every next centimeter
and a pentameter every next millimeter—all
mixed up with every – not *every* but *very*-
little scratching with my finger nail at tiny scabs,
peeling them away,; finding a little mole
or an old surgery stitch mark and titillate it.

Moods—hypothetical and subjunctive? Oh God!
There was only one mood like it is in free verse
Punctuated by cadences, mostly tactual, but verbal too.

Did the textual body understand the *schema* of my touch?
Yes, it did, I guess, for the quivering verbs and quailing nouns
all combined to put in a positive pulsating response—silent
but not without non-verbal vibrations.

Having passed this language lab course multiple times
With an 'A' grade, the sophomore in me is not sure
if he has learnt the grammar of the female body language.

One Love Letter

Difficult it is for me to burn these letters.
The hearth in my room is open; I sit in a chair on one side.
The heat reaches my loins two-fold—or so it seems.
I have already burnt quite a few—the dance
of flames sucks them in a burning orgy.
Orgy? What am I thinking? Orgy? I ask myself.

The letter in my hand is in English and it has
a familiar touch, a familiar scent, a taste
that makes me horny.

"Last night you were beside yourself", it records.
(The updraft holds it for a second, then turns into ash)
And suddenly I remember the night. Drunk I was.
Drunk with everything around—her body being the
first, last and foremost. What did I do
to merit this comment? Oh, I remember now.

"You said you'd give up your married life and
elope with me to Europe—where, you didn't know."
(The updraft holds it for a mini-second for me to read.)

Like a steel wire knotted into a human frame,
I sit up, uptight and taut.
Did I? O my God! Did I ever tell her that?
A drunken, drooling, jabbering fool
I must've been that night, how could I say that?
A wife, homebound, mother of three

A self-effacing simple woman, loyal and faithful?
And I? A false, faithless fool—a fake frump!

(The fire flickers in the hearth and the last pages
go up in updraft, spoof, spoof and spoof!)

Jai ho, Jai ho, Jai ho

(Hindi. Victory is mine, Victory is mine, Victory is mine.)

Grief rattles in the old cupboard of my skeleton.
Like a rattlesnake's tail end it is—warning me
that I should take care, or else . . . .
I understand what *or else* is for I have lived
with alternatives all my life. Off-center and
squint-eyed alternatives that are just surrogates
Not the causal originals.

The pompous gods, sitting in their high heaven
those who gamble with my fate
throwing the dice with my name on it,
are lazy, otiose and oily fatsos who don't know me.
"Oh, here he comes a cropper," says one
fetid fuck of a god—"the dice has come to a naught."
"There," says another of the trivial tribe, eroding
my gain with his toenail, "Write he will in his waspish
way his poems pooh-poohing gods, but
Can a weasel win a war—for his own weal?"
And he laughs heartily with his tummy tumbling.

I know the gods gamble with my fate
I know they are cheats of the worst kind
I know they do dice-ditching all the time
to make me lose my gains.
I know them through and through-
And yet I challenge them again and again.
In the end, I know, I will come out victorious.
Jai ho, jai ho, jai ho!

If Winter Comes

Horus non numero nisi Serenas. (I count only the sunny hours).

Motto on sundial quoted by William Hazlitt

Whoever wished
    for a high tide every day
    a full moon every night
    a sprightly spring always?

When I was a child of seven
    I wished precisely that
    and for me
    it was always the moment
    that determined the high, full and sprightly
    spring, moon and tide.

Scarlet of the maples could shake me down
    and frosty asters
    blue and violet—colors serene
    could make me dance in joy.

Never did I think of winter
    as a season of wailing winds
    of naked woods and meadows
    brown and bare.

This faculty I have no more
Neither do I wish for it
the springs or falls, summers or winters
the full moons or moony slivers
high tides or low times
are but things of the past

Born as babes we all are
and some remain so all their life;
others grow – ticking in them is the baby
with its nascent sun-lit face.
Still others grow and grow
till they're old and die.

Shall I be of that tribe?
I know and yet don't know
for it's still my thirtieth year
and forty years to go
I wish I still could feel
the West Wind itself reel
shake its snows and flounder
and let be off with December.

The woman with shaved head

"Schmoozing with a head is no nonsense matter,"
She said, and I kept quiet for I didn't know the word.
We went in the same car for our trip to the hospital;
she for her cryo surgery, I for my radiation.
Prostate cancer was my patrimony; head tumor was hers.

Can we trade our cancers? Once I asked.
You can, she said, for you also have a head, but I can't.
I said, I know, you don't have a prostate.
I have a uterus though, she said, but I wouldn't
trade it, no matter what.

We made small talk in our trips to and fro.
Head, she said, was a pumpkin—outside a shell
and inside pulp, just pulp. What is the prostate?
she asked. It is Adam's factory to produce sperms
I said, Sperms, you know, are little . . .

Another time she said, he wanted my tresses
So, I gave all my hair to him. The nurse was not happy.
She had shaved my head and wanted to keep the hair.
She kept all shaved hair in a drawer with a name tag.
He wanted my hair but not my uterus. I had become
pregnant, but he said, nothing doing, kill it.
The baby will inherit cancer. Damn it, she said
I don't want to talk about it.

The sperms get out of the prostate, she said
and then enter the uterus. Isn't it?
Man gives and woman receives . . . but then she
gives back a thousand-fold, a live baby! Isn't it?
Yes, I said, you are right.

We don't have to pick anyone today but you,
the driver told me. It was the last day of my therapy.
He added a little sadly, she expired last night.
She left a note for you with the nurse.
You can take it from her, he added.

A scrawled note on a lab slip the nurse gave me
And then the elderly nurse looked quizzically at me.
I could read only two words. Prostate . . . Uterus.

The Peeping TOM

Walking about late evening
around neighbors' houses lit
in darkened lanes unfit
even for me, on prowl
a naughty silent owl
I hoot and shoot a howl
scamper and turn the corner
to hide from an ugly neighborhood girl
she pulls down a blind to warn her
boy friend twice her age
pawing her in passion's rage.

A Peeping Tom I am
adept in my tomfoolery
all hunched up and unseen
I love to lurk, my keen
eyes glued to windows
I stoop to take a squint
at a bull and a cow in a kick
horns and hoofs and a hint
of something like a sick lick.

Passionless, I stand in th' shadow
like a hunter is all agog
in a swelling trance of fog
waiting for a query to show.
I've got to make a picture
with eyeballs dissolving in tincture.

Satyapal Anand

The Illusionist

Words in a tightly clamped fist
the illusionist historian opens it—and behold
one word flies out like a pigeon
then another, and then yet another
till we have a history book;
a self talking book that tells us all
nothing worthwhile was here in this
godforsaken land before Qasim set foot here.

Poor dear illusionist trembles in fear
for the master illusionist has taught him
only one trick—and after this first lesson
has shut in safe boxes words that depict
what was here in this godforsaken land
before Qasim—or whosoever had come here
from the great golden sandy land of Arabia.

His eyes, covered with the spider's web of fear
dare not open fully; his ears stuffed with cotton
cannot hear any other sound but Qasim's
and the talking book has a twisted tongue
wrapped around the leaves that repeat their truth.

Nothing was here, say the twisted leaves
except savages who drank cow's urine
burnt their widows on funeral pyres
keep untouchables subjugated
no philosophy, no religion, no knowledge
nothing but icon worship and stories of
the greatness of their gods.

Should he be told that the master illusionist
has been dead for years; the circus tent behind him
is an empty shell—and he should peel off spiders' webs
and take out cotton stuffing and then
see the world in its true colors.

He has been told, they say—but how would he do that
when the progeny of the master illusionist
in their millions is all brought up on th' first illusion?
They won't let him change the talking book, they say.

Nary a Word of Solace

Be niggards of advice on no pretence;
For the worst avarice is that of sense.
                    Alexander Pope

When my wife of fifty years died
I felt no sorrow, none to speak of.
Then came a day when others
With condolence messages came
Their hand on my shoulders
 Spoke words with icing of solace
Soothed I was with succor and cheer.
One said I must keep her picture clear
    A tiny one in my key ring—or, if not
On my work table, next to
my books, papers and computer.
That was the fittest way to keep her
Memory fresh as a winter flower
Due it was to her and you should give her.

    I kept a long, stricken mien
Throughout their words of solace
My face it was, indeed my face
That told them I was a hard-bitten
Frosty, hoar-man, so it was written
On my mug—they left me all but smitten.

Just five days after her last rites
I went for my stroll. We met on the way
She it was in person—and I in my *persona* myself.
Never she asked how I felt nor did I
Ask her how she was. We talked
Of stuff, great and small, mingled awry
And finally she went her way and so did I.

Back home I moved her picture
The one taken on deathbed serene and sad
From my work table—(I indeed was so mad
At the advice)—to the kitchen – her natural place
Hung it there and straightened my lengthy face.

We, the Memories

   Alone, forlorn and forgotten
Stand we all in a group with downcast eyes
We, the memories of the past that never turns back
Once it's gone.

   Once it is gone, it never looks back
Its shadows lengthen; its substance dissipates
Then a mere outline remains
And finally that also liquefies in the foggy cauldron
Memories sort themselves out
One by one.

   One by one they sort themselves out.
A teeny-weeny girlish boy plays on the Indus bank
His ball goes into the water—and splash
He goes after it; rises and sinks and rises again.
Throaty waves shriek like ghouls in agony
He gulps, rises, looks up in the sky
An early evening half moon stares back at him
The russet moon sways, lowers a long arm
Lifts him up—and throws him—ball and all
Back on the bank. Saved he was then—
Says the memory.

   Says the memory.
Another timid and bashful sliver of a tale
Told not by an idiot nor by a philosopher
But by the mere slip of a memory.
Stripped to the bone was the poor man
The loan-shark, the memory's grandpa

Swindled the man of his land, house and livestock.
Left alone he was with three kids to borrow more or starve.
Says the memory—the grandpa died of cancer
Tobacco-hookah had this in store for him.
"The upright shall dwell in the land
But the years of the wicked shall be shortened,"
Says the memory with a smirk.

Says she with a smirk
Another lovelorn lass of a memory recalls
How carefully cultivated love for a lad
Turned into hatred; her parents wouldn't let her
Marry the boy. She turned her heart into a rock.
Grew poison ivy instead of clematis in her garden
No healing fragrances, she said
Only stench and stink of disease and death.
And finally, as the memory recalls, she died a virgin.

She died a virgin—says another, but not the lad
Who was gored to death by her parents
As honor-killing was the tribal law,
And thereby hangs a tail, says the memory.

A tail, it hangs behind a cow
A cow reminds her of a cowboy
A cowboy of a herd and a horse
A horse of the Derby—and
Where would the chain stop?
Back to the tail or
Properly spelled a "tale".

We, the memories know all the tales
Stories and fables, rumors and fibs
Timid we are, old and forgetful—but
Ask us and we'll weave a night-long yarn.

The Three Facts

Birth and copulation, and death.
That's all the facts when you come to brass tracks.
T.S. ELIOT. "Fragments of an Agon." *Sweeney Agonists.*

(1926).

Sometimes I think of John the Baptist
Cheated by *aqua pura* that wasn't the *aab-e-zamzam*
Nor the holy water of the Ganges
Nor it was aqua vitae—the brandy as we know it.
Deceived he was by plain water and unmerciful love.

No baptism saves
Except through birth and copulation
And, finally, death.
In between the three mile stones is a vacuum
Filled by humdrum that is just hum and drum
No sound, no beat, no song.

Familiar, normal and medial
I think are scrambled parts of chaos
That fill this void—air in a balloon
Facts that are brass tracks too
Endure—not as an option
But as mandatory duties. John, the Baptist
Was supposed to know it.

Ars longa, vita brevis

"La guitarra hace llorar a los suernos"
Said Frederico Garcia Lorca to me;
A guitar is but a cheat
It makes human dreams sob;
Lost souls' sobbing escapes through its oval mouth.
It's wooden water traps their sighs
Like a tarantula that spins a huge star
So does a guitar."

  The sage from India
When I kept quiet, he chided me
With a dig he said, "Don't you agree with that?"
I lifted my eyebrows a little
"The enchanter art," he said, "is specious
Fake, a fraudulent friend. Not real.
Why don't you say something? O silent sage!"

  I said, "Silence is art, too, my friend Frederico.
Speech is silver; silence golden, they say.
Not that I'm in love with riches but . . ."

  He cut me short. "Oh, I know, sages love silence.
Maun brat—you call it—the fast of silence
You take a vow not to speak—isn't that art also . . .
The art of hiding your thoughts?"

  Mum I was, so he spoke again, "See here.
Sa'adi, the Persian sage had said
The tongue in your mouth is the key—
Yes, the key to the casket of your treasure.

The treasure of your mind – you open with it.
And unless, O sage, you open it
How would I know if you are a gem dealer
Or a peddler in trinkets. Speak you must, therefore."

   "Quite a long speech," I said,
But what about art and life? It is . . ."
He cut me short again. "Yes, I have the answer.
Both silence and speech are long,
Longer than life. Art stands no chance here."

Loneliness

   Great unbound sheaves of rain wander in the sky
Travelling skeins of water hit and dodge my window
Falling ribbons of silk furl out their wet colors
Parades of rain drive negro hordes of clouds ahead.
Alone I am at the window, waiting . . .

   . . . Free they are—unbound sheaves of rain
Black hordes of clouds that hit and dodge my window.
Do they know the meaning of loneliness?
Lonely for a *Shireen* for whom I once had nails of stone
And fingers of steel that could dig a canal with bare hands.
Lonely for Juliet who never could let fall her tresses
Down from her window for me to kiss . . .

   . . . Lonely for lustful love, I tell myself
No romance here, you the incorrigible poet
Lonely you are, but for her breasts
Warm porcelain taste of nipples on lips
Lonely you are, but for perfect spikes of
Imperishable eyelashes that touch your cheeks
Lonely, of course, you are and would still be lonely
When no rain clouds run their marathon
And no ribbons of silk fall from the sky.

Buddha in Shackles

In the **Buddha Temple** I prayed
Lit two candles – one a male body shape
The other a female figurine
A Yang-Yen combination it was.
Two smoke silhouettes rose—and then
Engulfed each other in arms.

This was Dharamshala, a town in India
The living Buddha had taken refuge there.
So it was that as Anand re-born, the first disciple
I went to meet him. No acquaintance was I
But he called me by my name. "O Anand, he said
Come and talk to me. Where's your Master?
Do the Chinese still keep him in prison?
Of course, you don't know, but I do.
The **dhyana-Zen** Master is in shackles.
The Master serves Lao-tse these days.
You and I—or the entire world—can't do anything.
Good bye, he said, go back to America
And forget about your last birth as Anand."

So, here I am again
A discarded membrane of Buddha's tongue
Not able to speak, but write I can
Embroider his words on paper, I will
And burn twin candles every day.

Satyapal Anand

A Virginal

Ezra Pound wrote a poem with this title in 1914)

    Don't go from me O April's tempting tipple
Th' swig swills and I sip a nip
As much of the booze as the nectar of her lip
Velvety round if taste can be touched with hand
Soft and sweet if touch is felt as taste.
Still warm and sheathed with comfy heat
I have the scent, the tangy, redolent flavor
Encapsulates in verdurous hair on my chest
April's tempting tipple let me savior
The magical tangy taste and the hypnotic best
Of her warm and salty sweat.

    Cloaked as 'with a gauze of ether'
Her 'slight arms' hold me tightly
I just love to be held in a scented tether
Mixing breath and all ever so sprightly
'Green come the shoots, aye April in the branches'
My April's in my arms, prove true all hunches
Of December, if winter comes
Can spring be far behind? No other choice.
So spring's here.
Shelley and Pound may both rejoice.

A baby named Aavi

(A lullaby)

A baby named Aavi
Third month ensuing
Trilling and cooing
Lies in his little bed
Fat legs spinning
Tiny tongue trilling
Chirps once, tweets twice
Flutters, fusses, gentle, nice
Howls, yowls, once twice.

Then happens something funny
Legs kick away the little toy bunny
A spew of water just rises awry
Gets jet stream right in the eye
Rises the little one's cry top high.
Mom comes running, "Why do you cry?
When your wee wee pees back at the sky!"

Cummings—you come

Cummings, you come
and be my guest
for a day
and a night
next morning too
if you can do
it in a day or two

Cummings, you come
if you have a story
tell it
in your honest words
without grammatical precision
and dishonest punctuation
the bane of cockney concision

Cummings, you come
like procrustes
we cut to size or
elongate to fit
our poetry bed
these grammarians
the procurators of
word treasures
have sat like snakes
guarding this wealth
of words

Cummings, come and see
capitalized i have just
two letters here
the c of your name
the e of English
for i love both
careful i have been
not to begin the
greek giant
procrustes name
with a cap
for he doesn't deserve one

Child on whose shoulders . . .

About to burst forth from his mouth
A shriek got muffled in his throat
Someone had put a massive hand on his mouth
He could only breathe through his clogged nose.

Eleven years old, he felt helpless
His hands were tied with a handkerchief
His mouth was stuffed with a towel
He had been turned on his belly
A big burly man was straddling him
Pulling his pajamas down
When it got entangled, he tore it off his feet.

Pitch dark it was all around
Enveloped in dead silence
Was the annexed outhouse where he slept
in the open courtyard on a rough cot.
He could now smell the man on top of him.
It was his cousin, ten years his senior.

He suddenly knew that the sky had burst open
His earth had countless leprosy patches
A five minutes' time span had put
a life-long festering wound in his heart.

Someone untied the handkerchief
Took out the stuffing from his mouth
Patted him on the back—and then
The ghoulish shadow just went out of the yard
And melted in the darkness.

He turned and got down from the cot
The white cotton sheet spread under him
Had a big round soiled patch in the middle
And his sinless mind had another splotch
Oozing out pus—white, leprosy-like
Wasn't it the child on whose shoulders
Many of my generation in Pakistan stand today?

(for Saqi
Farooqi)

Satyapal Anand

A dreamless sleep he has

Years after he died
a dreamless sleep he had—
no scene, no sound, no sense.

Time was when he was everywhere.
In a festive crowd he was the clown
In a marriage party he was the groom
Drunk he was almost every day
with beer cans, empty hotdog wrappers
orange peels and Cornish guts
raining like ticker tape all around him.
Drunk he was in the moon-full nights
when he kept awake
and the sunny days when he slept.

Just once he had a room
that he crept into from an open widow
when the owner had gone abroad.
Just once he slept in a bed
not like the stone-crib on the beach
heavy in sleep, full of dreams
headless men walking on footless legs
and kings throwing their crowns around
to play ball with courtesans.

He died and left, they say, a million to the city
in a bank locker with his Will (not of the wisp)
on one condition—and one, no more.

The city should have his statue erected
in the main park—with no name underneath.
Only then his million can be utilized.

   Years it took for them to debate
decline or accept his offer, and now
a clean, proud, tall, handsome HE stands.
A statue that always has a dreamless sleep.

Crossing the Road

A busy highway
Never-ending cars, bumper to bumper
Trucks, pick-ups, lorries
And the old man.

And the old man
Standing on one side
Peering, gazing, staring
One hand shading his eyes
Turning his head right and left
No let up does he espy
No break in the fast flowing traffic.

Takes a step
Turns back hastily
The car driver curses
Shows a fist—zooms by
The trucks seem to sing a song
Come up
Old man
Come up
Old man
Get killed
Get killed.

Stuffs his ears with his fingers
No way to get across
No way to get home
All others have gone across
His mom, his dad, his wife.

No way to go and join them.
How might they have crossed?
I don't know—but
There might've been a break
A break in *this* traffic?
Impossible.

Black exhaust chokes him
Noise makes him deaf and dumb
The truck song continues
Unabated
Now louder
And faster
Come up
Old man
Come up
Old man
Get killed
Get killed.

Takes a step again
Down the pavement
On the road
Shuts his eyes tight.
Takes another step
And another
And another.

Suddenly he feels someone
Holding his hand
 guiding him across
A woman, his own mother
As she looked
fifty years back
guides him thru' the traffic.

"Come, my little child,"
she coaxes him,
"Hold my hand
You will cross safely!"

Icarus, the Second

Daedalus, O my father, you don't know
My strength and speed far exceeds
The heat of the sun: I will go as an eagle
Fly out of Crete and escape certain death.

Daedalus, they say, knew but he wouldn't
Discourage his son, the warrior, brave and fearless.
Death was certain, indeed, and Icarus died
Plunging back to earth, the wax melted
Wings gone—and what he left for the world
was a story of indomitable courage
and cruel fate poised against each other.

Icarus, the Second—likewise
Grew wings and crossed the seven seas
reaching the New World—a Columbus reborn.
He had no father to make wings for him
No one to glue them with wax to his body
No one to give him courage.

Yet he flew and flew and flew
Escaped both his Crete that was India
And his fate that he never was friendly with.
No one shall ever remember him
For he leaves no story behind—
of success much less than one of failure.

Satyapal Anand

Pathetique

*Mozart composed a sonata and Tchaikovsky a symphony with
this title*

How can one get a new life-span of the statue
Of the sea god in the depths of the ocean
Where no one can see it and worship it?

Nymphs alone leave pathetic notes of the
Aquatic musical instrument *jaltarang*- mixed
With Tchaikovsky's symphony or Mozart's sonata.

Our bodies gone, our bones bleached
Carve an ossified white cross from them
Summon ospreys for bone breaking
Why white? For Red Cross ostensibly
is less a cross and more a crunching crescent.

Torture the tortured you may
Their cries in purgatorial butchery are stifled.
Dante, poor soul, never himself understood
The taste of torture—which has the end result
for both the torturer and the tortured.

Pull out the nails one by one
Crush each finger in a grinder
Taking your time in gouging out an eye
Half an hour? Or more? Depends
On how much you enjoy the surgical procedure.

Leave be. Better methods there are
In the world today—without blood
Nay, without even a mark on the body.

Hallucinatory drugs—right in the arm
Deafening sounds crushing the essence of being
Pangs of punishment in brain
Gethsemane glut of mental garroting
Agony and anguish deep inside
The mind lacerated—martyrdom denied.

Pathetique? Yes, psychotically drilled
Making the recipient a *non compos mentis*
Say the Delphic doctors in army's pay
Medically gifted, judicially penurious.
Don't think only of a Nazi prison!

The Night I Didn't Kill Myself

    Drove my car right to the shore
The Bay was wrapped in a century-long silence
People fishing, gossiping, strolling, kissing
They were all there as on all days
This day, the silence was inside me.

    Occasion? None. Provocation? None.
Stimulants? Many. One being to see how I drown.
Shall I sink like a stone or a
Gelid galleon full of iced seafarers?
Curiosity? Yes. Who will fish my body out?
And how? Will they hoist me with a crane?
 A masked marine netting my corpse
And pulling me up with ropes?
Maybe, half-eaten by fish I become
Lighter than water and float on the surface.

    Too many were the possibilities.
I got out of the car, took a few steps
Went back into the car
Opened my thermos bottle
Drank some coffee, stale but steady
And then? And then?
I chose not to kill myself that day.

Mutual Relationship

"I hate myself," I spoke unconcernedly
Someone heard me, the wind it was
And it asked me to say it once again.
"I hate myself!" This time I said it loudly.

The sky it was or the wind or the stars
I don't know who accosted me thunderously.
"Your own self also hates you
In the same measure as you hate it.
Know it once for all, O the ignoramus fool
The equation of mutual relationship
Between self and self is always congruent.

The Lone Pilgrim Woman

It was but a single ferry on the river bank
The pilgrims, men and women, both stepped
On the deck and walked below
Into its cavernous entrails for their pilgrimage.

It was early in the morning
The breeze blew from the river to the dry land
Palm trees were rubbing sleep out of their eyes
A few sea birds cawed and swooped and fished
It was all quiet in the crowd that went up the deck
One by one, men, women—and even children,
A slow, silent procession it was.

When all had embarked, the ferry gave a whistle
The engines started with a push or two—and
There was no one on the railing, but . . .

But a lone elderly woman—all by herself
Standing next to the railing
Peering high and low in the distance
Shading her eyes against the sun behind the palm trees
Looking for something or someone she was.
She wished to see someone running head over heals
Towards the river bank, maybe shouting,
"Hey, wait a minute.
I also have to go. Don't leave me stranded here!"
But there was no one, no one at all.
Only the palm trees and the wind and the birds.

Finally, she turned
Ready to go down from the deck
Disappointed she was for her husband was left behind
And then she saw to her amazement
that each one on this last pilgrimage
Men, women and children, went unaccompanied, alone.
No one had a consort.

One Square Inch of Silence

    Tumultuous thoughts
Riotous, mutinous, seething with unrest
A savage dance, turbid and turgid
Of pent up feelings
Inside my mind, a storm unspent—
It has made me a crazed creature.
Can't hear my own voice; impervious
I have become
Even to a shout or a holler.

    Noise, tumult-a deafening din
Is all my lot—if I could get
One square inch of silence in this sea
I would jump into it and never
Come out of even as a bubble.

A mere thirty bucks it was

Walks alone the ugly unctuous poet
An oily tongue glistens in the mouth that wets his lips
Five feet four, an elfin cabbalist
Unbuttoning his shirt but zipping up his fly
A smile, damned sly, short of being shy,
He goes to the poets' corner in the bar
Orders a drink—and waits.

Waits for one of his tribe
That comes soon enough, a smirk and a smile
Stamped and fixed on corpulent lips
Sebaceous, oily and greasy yet tall
Takes out a tubby-pudgy wallet—and then
Asks for his wares – and waits.

There's no wait time
For the elfin cabalist has it ready
An envelope white
In front of him right
Two poems, he said—and two more—he said
Are yours for a mere thirty bucks.

The exchange done
They button their shirts
Zip their flies and go out, hand in hand.

Don Juan? Casa Nova?

(Based on the diary of a dear departed friend)

One hundred? Did you say, one hundred?
That is One-Zero-Zero?
His girl friend, the beauty from Isfahan is aghast.
Did you really say, one hundred? She asks again.
And when prompted by pride and a little hubris
He tells her that she is the sixtieth on the list
She first snickers, then laughs loudly—
Lights a cigarette, takes a puff or two
And then utters a Farsi sobriquet that could mean
Lecher or luptuary or *roué*
Or all three rolled together
And when he suggests, one more word
Don Juan, she has no comment, for she has
Never heard the name, so innocent she is.

The memory lane is dark
Winds its way many times and there are
Shades and silhouettes that
He doesn't recognize as women he had met
And had been with them
Loved them and left them—or they had left him.
Difficult it is and laborious—for him to remember it all.
Audition of conversation, geometry of lips dissolving in yours
Eyes and eyelashes, mystery of neck merging down into
The cleavage—and then, the cleavage itself!
Its soft and satiny touch or cold rubbery feeling—
These are the things he remembers

In isolation from others, alone or unique
But the woman as a whole—only bits and pieces
Or as a tick-marked number in a catalogue.

Fifty-nine they were, before Mona from Iran
All younger or his own age or, well, a few years older
But all he treated as children rather than friends.
دشت نوردی Mona asks him   *A memory walkway?* (Farsi)
"Are you reminiscing?" "I am," he says—and
As if that is a sign of dismissal, she picks up
Both her bag and herself, and just walks she away.

He just can't count, indeed, not the exact number
But many were from his own country India
Jet black, swarthy, brown, light colored, palely white
Concise, abridged and precise like an outline of a thesis
Or a verbosely expanded – big, thick voluminous journal.
Habituating, rehearsing, acclimatizing—it was
A period of drill and practice for Casa Nova of India;
The prime matches had yet to come.
So, no steps counted, at all, on his memory walkway.
No memory walkway, Ms. Mona, except for
A name as a tag and a face as a label.

Velutinous she was, covered with golden hairs
On her body, Russia's Czarina Matushka
the one who had met him in Delhi
And had gone to Simla with him.
Norway's Maria, one who had said
The frozen loins of the North are no match
For you, O the virile son of India.
Suddenly his mind's mirror reflects an image
Rounded and thick buttery lips, the upper one
In particular, the Queen of Sheba from Africa
Who had told him that two races become one only
When their skin pigments mingle and merge.

For that, she thought, a pilgrimage to India
Can only be done inside his hotel room.

Fatima was Portuguese and lived in New York
A baby-sitter, she would get food and wages both.
"My profession's such," she had told him
"I've to make the babies' dads also happy . . .
I mean, if I want to make an extra buck or two."
From his wallet she never took more than ten.

Kim, who had been introduced to him by a friend
Telling him that she was a Chinese but she hated
Her flat face and nose . . . All her family was killed
When she was a baby. No kith or kin she has now.
A staunch Buddhist, she likes India very much.
Take her there and keep her . . . for keepsake
If nothing else.

And the underage Sophia of London
One who had told him a sad story. Her father, she said,
Was a Paki but her mom was British. Needs money,
for college . . . She knew postures that only whores know.
The two were together for three continuous days
A forty-pound a day contract that was.

And Sheila of Canada! The Sheila—he wrote in his diary.
The Sheila for this name has occurred thrice before, he wrote.
There were three more, all in India. The first one?
Oh, the first one! She was not even fifteen, a school kid
Who had entangled him. Not he, but her. Oh, God!

Time? Three decades!
Distance? Three continents long and wide!
Time and distance
Two dimensions that merge in a quaint way.
The mind doesn't know for sure which is which

And what is what and who is who.
"Why do I begin the first entry with Mona?"
He asks himself and then answers, it is
Because she was the only one who smoked
While he didn't. What a reason? He wonders.

   Beyond sixty? Well, yes! Writes he.
A Casa Nova or a Don Juan never reaches the end of a list.

Satyapal Anand

Recuerdo

Descending the plane's steps manually she smiled
Gave me her handbag to hold, for she herself held a baby
And a five-year old too who held her finger. Another bag
Hung from her shoulder. So it was that I came handy.

A great fog bank advanced on Heathrow
Alighting we were on open ground
Wet and slippery with rain overnight
No gate to park the huge jet—We had to walk.

It happened then; she slipped—and fell.
The baby I caught in midair like a ball
The kid behind rolled over her—safe
Didn't cry at all, helped the limping mom up
On her feet—and seemed well, at least for a sec.

Quick came down a flight-attendant
Thank god, your family's safe
He said to me, helped her with the fallen bag.
We walked. The baby smelled nice.
It was a cozy bundle I held
And her bag, too; till we reached
The baggage claim, no one said a word.

Then it was that she spoke in Spanish
Sustantivo, Gracias! Just two words I understood
She took the sleeping baby from my arms
Said *gracias* again, reached over—and
Kissed me full on the lips; a warm, wet kiss it was.

Sustantivo baso, she said, recuerdo.
Es todo un caballero, She told her five-years old.

   I carried the kiss back home
Still wet, still sweet—and then found my Latin dictionary.
Recuerdo meant a memento, a gift.
So the kiss was a gift to remember her by.
Es todo un caballero, meant: 'He's a real gentleman.'
That was the explanation to her son.

Conversation it indeed was!

All my answers I had kept
Simple, easy to understand.
Difficult and long-winded were
All her questions.

Tiny, puny things
Little half-formed sentences
She always had loved
Took them in her lap like kitten
Kissed and smooched them
Patted and caressed them.
Now they bored her
She felt nauseated
With short, meaningless cooing
Unworthy of her they seemed to her
Not serious enough.

Something had happened.
I was still the same old self
Childish and jocular—or both.
She had grown
Grown as a serious
High-class, highly bred
Woman of the world.
The all-powerful manager of a corporate body.
I continued to be a childlike
Adolescent, ready to die
If she ever asked me to—
And she, no longer was the one
I loved, admired—nay, worshipped

The very earth she stepped on – and she?
As it were, never walked on earth now.

  All my answers I had kept
Simple, easy to understand.
Difficult and long-winded were
All her questions. The conversation was a still birth.

Satyapal Anand

The Ultimate Question

A drip in the right arm vein
Another in a vein at the back of her hand
Another—and yet another—in other body parts.
Wires and cables, meters and clock faces
All blink, sometimes rubbing their eyes
Sometimes plainly staring or blinking.
A giant spider has woven a web around her
A hundred-headed sea serpent has coiled itself
Around her. No let up, no freedom from this bondage
For her, I know; she is in the Intensive Care Ward.

Calm, quiet, dead silence
Indeed more dead than silent is the ward.
No one breathes; no one is alive
I know that's not true, but it looks to be so.
A subdued footfall is heard
Of a nurse walking by or a ward boy
Seems to have lost his way back to the living world.

I sit on a stool by her bed—my sister's bed
Twelve years my senior, she mothered me as a baby.
Is it she on the bed? I ask myself
There's a body, more dead than alive
My sane self tells me. Known by a name
She is till today, but maybe, tomorrow
That name is also forgotten.

Who is that? A being or spirit or power or whatever?
The one that can give back to my mom-like sis

Her real self—self that she had kept in tact
For three scores-minus-ten years?

  What is that? The breath that comes and goes?
A soul or spirit that inhabits the frame of a body?
Where does it come from?
Where does it go? Whence? Back to where?
Does it ever come back to see its old home, the body?

  Sitting next to her bed on a stool
In the Intensive Care Ward—I continue to ask
These silly questions.

A Memory Flash

Unpredictable as a memory flash
I think of myself—a dandling boy-man of fifteen
Halfway up the slippage of my youth.
Back in my village in India
shack-to-shack-combined roofs—flat
mud plastered, they were, easy to go from one to another
down the open stairs and right into the courtyard.
One did it all the time, if one had to do some
backyard buccaneering prompted by
Bacchus and Cupid combined.

Does my memory flash include oval focuses?
No, it doesn't. What it does is an acutely felt
self-inflicted epidural, injected right into the spine
shuddering ensuing and lasting for hours.

A dandling boy-man, I said, and I was no Orpheus
in search of Eurydice in hell but I did go to one
almost every night. Two were there, a mom and her
daughter—not divine but earthy, sweet and silly.
The lass it was, my own age, who took me
once in the *cul-de-sac* behind and told me to come at night
and we'd do it again. So I went and we were together
but then mom came and joined us in the bed –
no questions asked.

Just a mere cruddy, I never asked why
but came to know from gossip buzzing like flies
that she was an abandoned wife, left high and dry
without even a divorce, the hubby a run-away thief.

The daughter was just ten then—
and now my own age she was, a girl-woman.

   No gleam without a maggot or a firefly
Said the neighbors—and added a wise saw
"You can't be a pea in two pods."
And my grandpa who ruled more than a mere roost
Packed me off to a town to study and told me to
stay put even in my summer vacation.

   Could I sneak back for a day? The bus plied
once a week and took nine hours. It was an Odyssey.
   Three years past I came back for a week. Found
nothing. The house was locked and shuttered
No inmates there. I didn't even ask neighbors
where and when and why? By then I, the boy-man
had gone up the youth slippage path, become a man
and had found greener pastures in the city.

Satyapal Anand

A Mongrel Snarl

Friends we were to become, it seemed
the dog and I. We played.
A bulky beast, massive and mature he was
From the neighborhood and roamed at will.
The first day we met, he came running
Groveling at my feet; salivating, he looked up
and whimpered. Am I acceptable? He seemed to ask.
I stopped, patted his head and said audibly,
You're welcome, my friend.

That should have been all
But he groveled a little more and then –
He lifted his leg and peed at my shoes
—a mere squirt but messy it was
grimy and sloppy—an insult more than effrontery.
I turned a step back and stamped my feet
A mere ostentation to let the frowzy fluid flow free . . .

The dog just smiled—showing his canines
And a mouthful of other tearing equipment.
Beasts don't laugh; only men do, say the sane
And I knew, my stomping meant a threat
And his pure-breed smile, if I stayed long,
Would turn into a mongrel snarl.
So, with my tail in my legs
I backed slowly and then walked off-stage.

Your hates, fostered in falsity

No, not a love letter I write, my love
a missive meandering through mongrel streets
of penmanship, it is. Just take it at will, not as a pill
to cure your migraine.

Victorian (or Georgian) English I use
for a purpose, you know. Only when I want to play
false to myself, not to the addressee of the missive.
False to myself doesn't mean false to you, my love.

Only the crazy sweetness, I write, I know
and stare at what I wrote till the page's blurred
but all along it is your visage that the eyes see
it isn't blurred; mesmerizes me with its mystique.

Now that you've cast aside me, an old apron,
what can I do but hold my silence, keep mum
and nibbling my nails at my own naiveté
make myself an un-noteworthy nothing, O dear.

Fostered in falsity your hates still hold
while I, like an empty balloon
void and devoid of air, lie crushed
—a mere scrap of tattered rubber.

(Written in 1956)

Galatea, O Galatea!

I

- What a statue it was!
  Its facial contours, features, total profile
  curves and slopes, the entire form and figure
  emerged from the stone slab
  as if they had been at rest there for centuries.

- What a look she had!
  Face, eyes—the dawning color of sunrise on cheeks
  bright shade of a playful smile on curved lips
  brownish black—a full head of hair
  stone converted to silk—a statue made of silk and stone.

- What a figure she had!
  With the sharp strokes of my cutting tools
  like a white flower opening its petals in slow motion
  her silvery soft body had blossomed in the air.
  A veteran cutter and carver, even I thought
  the statue would open its eyes, wake up
  smile at me and say, I am now alive, my master.

II

- A benediction from Aphrodite, my patron goddess
  or a miracle of my own art it was—I don't know, but
  when I saw my own handiwork, the carved statue,
  the only prayer that rose from my heart was—
  indeed, if this woman carved in stone were to come alive,

a live, warm, breathing, talking goddess in human form,
what wouldn't I give for such a gift?
I would worship her like the goddess she is.
I would kiss the very earth she walked on.

* The prayer, indeed, the prayer
rose like an impassioned plea from my heart
reached the portals of gods' mansions in the heaven
and lo, and behold, . . .

* And lo, behold!
Aphrodite just opened her petal-like lips
and said, "Let it be!" and it was done.
The fairy, the goddess, the icon of my worship
did indeed become a woman.

* Her face, her eyes, her golden tresses, lips
and that silver-white, velvet-soft body
breasts like lotuses, a neck that would shame a swan
fragrant breath—they were all for me:
for me alone was her youth and her beauty
for me alone, let me repeat, and for no one else.

* Her worship was my sacred duty
to adore and admire, to adulate and revere –
that was my sole reason of being
my love was my duty first and foremost.
She was my goddess; I was her worshipper.

III

* For an artist to become a worshipper of his own
art piece? Never was heard a story like this by me.
It wasn't natural or normal; wasn't even conventional.
Bizarre and freakish it was; no norm or nuance allowed it

Satyapal Anand

And yet here I was, an atypical creator
worshipping his own creation. Topsy-turvy, eh?

- A slave—nay, a willing slave, like a canine cur
  I would follow her everywhere, do her bidding every time,
  went against my own better nature to obey her commands,
  did everything within my means to please her. Such was my
  devotion; a reverent worshipful slave I had become.
  No longer I was-the old Pygmalion of the sacred order of art
  But a new Pygmalion of the order of a female deity.

IV

- The idyllic canonization could go on indefinitely
  but for the ignominy heaped upon me.
  How long? How long could one endure this?
  The artist is told he had already carved his best
  Namely herself. No more now! Throw away your tools
  and just do what I ask you to do.

- Ill-fated was I; ill-favored by my own creation.
  What indeed was she? A mere woman,
  a mere good looking female
  fallacious and specious –, nay, illogical.
  Give up my most treasured art? Shall I?
  Uncultivated she was—a mere body
  lacking refinement, lacking subtlety
  lacking finesse, lacking discretion.
  Fussy and finicky she was aplenty
  But without sophistication—a beautiful
  doll, an ugly soul.

V

- Do I want her dead?
Crushed, crunched, and splintered—a heap of dust?
No, how could I even think of it?
My love she was, a part of my aesthetic self, my creation
Indeed, so. But what should I do?
Ask her to be kind and reasonable—considerate
kind to me?

- I did—and the result was negative.
No juice of mercy flowed in those lovely lips.
Abuse, harm and hurt bubbled in her words.
Love? A word she didn't know – didn't care to know.
Understanding or logic had no acquaintance with her.
Just a plain stone idol with a heart of stone and no soul.

VI

- Galatea, O Galatea! Once I hit my head
against your nearest stone column. You laughed.
I cried like a babe. You snickered.
I lay on the ground in front of you. You were unmoved.
I said—what should I do? You said: Be as you are.

- Galatea, O Galatea! You know you are not real
An art piece like you is once-in-a-lifetime achievement,
you know this also. What you don't know is that I have,
though not often, destroyed my own creations.
My hammer is my mute witness. When I do not like
my own creation, I let it stay for a day or two
and then destroy it. I have done it before. I can do it again,
but I will not destroy you. You will live.

Satyapal Anand

VII

- You will live, Galatea.
  No, you will not live, Galatea.
  You will live, Galatea.
  No, you will not live, Galatea.
  Live.
  Not live.
  Live.
  Not live.
  Live, not live. Live, not live. Live, not live. Live, not live.

- I, Pygmalion, the creator of Galatea
  A name that resounds in four corners of the earth
  to whom even gods come for favors
  who has loved life and worshipped life
  is going to shatter his created life into pieces.
  O gods in heaven, witness what I am about to do.

- Forgive me, Aphrodite
  forgive me, my patron goddess
  What I am going to do is unheard of in human history
  but will reverberate for all times to come.

The Rope Walker

A rope, sturdy, strong and tight
tied to two steel poles a life-time across
the narrowest bridge—One, the Islamic faith
visualized all souls crossing.

My walkway of life is this rope
sturdy, strong, tight and taut—connecting
two extremities, two moments in the flow of time
my birth and my death—the void in between
this rope bridge overspreads—a long distance, indeed.

Bare-footed I am and I stand sturdily on the rope.
One foot ahead and one foot behind –
I hold the rope in the crook of my big toe and
look behind to see how much distance I've covered.
Then look ahead to envision how far I have to go.
Maybe, I have covered one half of a distance.
Looks like it, I tell myself, but I don't know for sure.

I was but an innocent babe when I began doing it.
Learnt to do it the hardest way, falling often,
hurting myself, getting punished for it, too.
Why didn't I learn to walk on the ground?
The safe and solid, plain earth was there—and yet
with a hateful glance at it, I had said: No!
Nothing doing! O my elders, I'll walk on a rope,
do something that no one has done before.

Satyapal Anand

Why did I choose rope walking? I ask myself.
I don't know, I tell myself, but now it is too late—
too far gone on my journey I am to turn back and begin anew.
I'll walk the rest of my distance, high up, on the rope.

You are the actor on the stage, not one of the audiences
Finally, I hear my inner self tell me.
Your preordained fate it is. You either do it—or die.
You can't walk on the earth like ordinary mortals.
A special breed you are! Bravo! Keep it up!
How much distance is left? I again ask myself.

The Gorilla Pass-Out Parade

"Hip-Hip Hurray!"
"Up and high ! Smite hip or thigh!"

Like all other gorillas, he too hurls his cap in the air
The conical cap that he wears especially for this day,
And shouts—hurting the ears of others nearby
"Hip-Hip Hurray! I've earned my army commission!
I will be an officer on the front.
Fight for my country, I will—and
Kill our enemies—the damned humans!"

"Hip-Hip Hurray!"
"Up and high! Smite hip or thigh!" he shouts again.

All around him, gorillas hurl up their caps high
Shout as if they're going to the battle front in a moment.
Tightening their fists, waving in the air
Singing with the army band—"Long Live Gorilla-land",
They come out of the Convocation Hall.

Hypognathous apes all, they celebrate.
Brothers, sisters, aunts and uncles
Friends and neighbors—they are all there
Toasting them, hailing and extolling them.
Champagne corks pop—and the sound
They mimic with their tongues.
Drinking to their health and wishing them
Victory over the damned humans.

Satyapal Anand

Inside the hall that is empty now
Scattered on the floor are conical caps
Empty bottles, corks, soiled paper towels, straws
A couple is still hugging in a corner.
(Kissing is a human curse! They say)
The gorilla pass-out parade comes to an end.

The Sign on the Monitor

What indeed was the sign?
The sign had just appeared on the monitor—and then
Sliding fast from one corner to another
had just disappeared in its cavernous belly.
It was there a moment ago and then it wasn't.
I know the word very intimately, he said to himself
as if he wanted a reason to say something.
Its contours I know very well, don't I?
He reaffirmed and then again put an interrogative.
Don't I know the word? Yes, I do, he said again.

The computer was still there, the monitor was lit up.
He let his fingers tap the keys in a well versed order.
Looked at the monitor again but it was a blank blue sheet.
The sign had gone deep into the computer's belly.

Come, he asked himself, let's guess what it was!
He rubbed his aching eyes, thought for a while.
What in the world was it? What, indeed, what?
Was it the Cross, the Christian symbol?
Was it a *halaal*, the slice of moon, a Muslim sign?
Was it a Jew sign? A Hindu sign?
I just can't surmise, but I know it'll reappear.

He lifted his blind eyes to the monitor
As if he hoped that when this icon returns
He would get his eyesight back.

Satyapal Anand

Can One Riddle Solve the other?

Water—a major ingredient
A tiny fire flame, a fistful of earth
A mere breath of air—going in and coming out
The tiniest atom of ether, substance of heaven
Gleaming, glistening, glittering
A mere hint of luminescence
Water, fire, earth and air make a physical form
Added to it is a ray of light from heavens
A palpable figure, a physical frame . . .
Yet an unsolved riddle!

On all sides—above, below, front and back
Right and left, inside-out, outside-in
Boundless, eternal, infinite
Wearing their ether-overalls
Inhabitants of galaxies, cosmic highways and byways
Suns, planets and moons
Evident, visible, clear—a universe . . .
Yet an unsolved riddle!

Can one riddle solve the other?

Shrinkage

Emaciated body
Lean and lank—scrawny
Sparse and spare – exiguous
A loose gown hanging from emaciated shoulders
Raw-boned figure tottering on bird-feet . . .

Looks back at me from the mirror—this image
Masquerading, feigning, posture making
Slowly turning on one foot to show a side pose
An actor—a jokester
It suddenly asks . . .

You haven't recognized me, ah?
Time—I am.
Do you recall when you had last seen me?
You were sturdy as a stone pillar
A steel column—stout and strong
Solid, sound and strapping you were.
Look in the mirror again
Recognize me . . .

No one was there
My own reflex ion stared back at me
My own normal self
Emaciated body
Lean and lank

Satyapal Anand

Sparse and spare—exiguous
A loose gown hanging from shoulders
Tottering on bird feet.
A robot with loose limbs.

The Way Back Home

There was a park on the side of the road
I had just come out of my house for a walk
Grassy, green trees, flowers, birds, children
Flower beds, *flora and fauna* (the term escaped me.)

Benches there were – many on all sides
Their walking days over
Old people sat and rested their tired limbs
Pale, emaciated faces
Folds and creases going from nowhere to nowhere
Women and men—some care-taking nurses also.

Children played
Dogs ran about bidding their masters' orders
Fetching rubber balls in salivating mouths
A lad flying a home-made kite shouted in hilarity.
Sun, like an old tired wanderer, walked
at the horizon rim, about to enter portals of day's doom.

Tapping my walking stick I pass by—
Think, maybe, I could sit on a bench, relax
There! There is a bench unoccupied, I coax myself.
In an even measure of yes's and no's
I look around—and finally tell myself
Shouldn't I keep on walking?
My trip from one home to another
Doesn't seem to be much longer.

Satyapal Anand

Who is the Grave-Digger?

Look around! Look around and ask!
Who is the grave digger? Where is he?
The corpses that lie all around—do you see?
Who is going to bury them?
Flocks of vultures flying overhead—don't you see ?
Let me ask once again and again
Who is the grave digger? Where is he?

Who were the killers of these innocent people?
Are you all deaf and dumb? Why don't you speak?
You know and yet you don't speak. Why?
Look at the dead bodies—scattered like fallen logs
All around the field they are—half covered by grass already.
Some are without heads, some without legs or arms.
Look at this here! The abdomen open, entrails hanging out
Entangled, round and round like a grape vine, blood-red!

They say in the fable, a crow had told. Whom?
Abel or Cane?—How to bury a murdered brother.
Come on all of you, let's find a crow, if there is
Ask him what to do with hundreds of corpses.
Not improbable, it is either Abel or Cane
That has killed so many of his brothers.
Don't ask me, O brother, the murderers' names
Just ask this--
Who is the grave digger? Where is he?

How does he recognize himself?

How do I distribute him into breed and ilk?
The parts of the man known as Satyapal Anand-
how do I divide him into known or unknown lineages?

His face and forehead are his father's
gift to him. So is the light color of the skin.
His mother's part is evident more in his mind
than his body: benevolent, benignant and humane
these are his mother's traits.

On which personality shelf would I place
his grandparents-maternal and paternal?
Is there a place for any earlier generations?
The great-grand, the great-great-grand and so on?
Faces, features, contours, height, hair—
Doesn't all this constitute a racial stock?
Who gave what and when to him and how much?
Will he ever know?

Race, stock, breed, tribe?
Class, kind, group, clan?
A hodge-podge mixture
A blend, a muddle, a maze
Hundreds of thousands of people—all related
A million steps from bottom to top
where he stands on his parents' shoulders
and they on theirs and they on theirs.

Purity?
Aryan? Jew? Caucasian?
Black, Arab, Nomad, Indian?
What else would you have?
All a blended assortment, a miscellaneous medley.
How does he recognize himself?

Mona Lisa—Where is she?

Mona Lisa was right there on the wall
An expensive print highlighted by a hip frame
Mona Lisa she was—her secretive rictus
Neither a smile nor a smirk—a mystery
A half-budded flower still asleep on the lips.

Come on, speak up, Mona! I would implore her
Share with me the secret of your smile
I won't tell anyone, I swear by you
You, the most precious possession I have,
At least in this room, I ask this question every day.

A conjecture or something akin to reality it was
On some nights I felt her lips were open
The half-bud had budded fully.

A conjecture it was I know, for she was
The same conundrum in the morning
Her secret self never open to anyone but
To her creator, maybe, not even to him.
He had immortalized just a single moment
In her mood sequence; one single moment in time.
How could he interpret it for posterity?

She came down from the wall one night.
I was asleep, but I got up trembling in fear.
D' Vinci's masterpiece was standing on the floor
A dilapidated old woman with a toothless mouth
Her face, her cheeks, her forehead had deep furrows.
Her hair had turned to the color of dust

Satyapal Anand

She was a pale, lifeless caricature of herself.
And yet to an art connoisseur like me
She was the best D' Vinci could have painted
But, unfortunately, did not.

Grief-stricken as I was, she smiled at me.
A sad effort it was; it showed an empty shell of a mouth.
It must've been only once as an art piece
But she did endeavor to smile.
Her message I understood fully. She said silently
I hope, my secret will not go out of this room.
I nodded—and she walked out.

It is morning now
As usual I rub my eyes to look at the wall.
I rub my eyes again for she is not there
The wall is bereft of her picture.

The Four Elements

Come along, my grieving self, we'll trace her
in the warp and woof of the four elements.

We beckoned the air
It nodded and said—
Oh No! she was but a whiff of my own breath
that I took back. She had borrowed it from me.

A quizzical glance towards a bubbling spring
brought a whooshing answer—
I don't know where she is at the moment.
The water part of her was a common property
She had borrowed it.
So, why grieve you if it was taken back?

Suddenly, the swirling dust spoke
She's with me. She's in my lap. Here she lies.
But do understand that it is not the person
You're looking for. With me she's just dust and ashes.

It was an angry, fire-spewing sun
At the horizon, about to set. He said in a brimstone voice
Don't accuse me, O mortals!
It was a tiny, puny candle light that I absorbed.
Nothing more there was with the dying woman.
Where is that now?
Nowhere you don't see me, and everywhere
you see me.

Fruitless it is to look for her now
She's divided into her four elements
the air, the earth, the water and the sun.

(Written after my wife's death)

The Wounds of My Soul

Countless are the wounds of my soul.
These lacerations bleed all the time.
Stabs and gashes of verbal insult are
scratches and cuts, equally painful.
Sores, full of pus, a visible record of undue hurts
wreck me day in and day out.

A self-respecting man, I would never
exhibit these wounds as laurels won
or battle scars of mortal combats.

The blood-stained cotton and bandages,
all discarded dressings I bury in my heart
and hope that my next-door neighbors don't see
any sign of my affliction.

These, my past hurts, the wounds of my soul
are mine—and mine alone!

(1957)

Satyapal Anand

Libidinous Lollipop

A column of cold stone – sleek, silken and smooth
Exquisitely attractive girls—scantily dressed
Dancing around, touching it with tongues
Licking, flicking and lapping
A lickerish, lustful, lave orgy of sex and valor
Two thousand years ago in Rome
Thousands of men clap watching.

Shiva linga, the tip of a stone icon
As if protruding from the earth itself
Installed in the inner sanctum of a temple –
Washed ceremoniously with water and milk
by married women—young and comely
seeking benediction for a male issue.
Washed with hands, caressed, bussed, patted
Loved reverentially—the hard *linga* of stone,
Stands upright in all temples in India.

You are no different, O worshipful sorceress
When you hold it like a scepter in both hands
Enwrap its amber jewel head with your tongue
thus urging its blessings—and
Making it puff up its manhood two-fold.
What you do is the same ritual
As done by women in Rome yesterday
And women in India today.

Contracts of Feigned Glory

Catches a favorable gust of wind
It soars, the kite—and you, the child in you
Think that you are flying high
A mighty high-flying hawk
Your puny ego is puffed—at least for that moment
You look down upon the entire world.

Behold, the master is flying high!
You seem to be shouting to the world at large.
Never could you fly your kite-self this high
When you were really a child—but now
When your adult-self is a grown up child
You think you can go higher than others'.

The tame kite is like a trained falcon
One tied with a string to your finger
The other but a cordless extension of the hunter
Both are contracts of feigned glory
With your puny self that can't fly.

Satyapal Anand

To a friend I met recently

You are all the women I met before
rolled into one. Where were you?

Now that I think of the past
All bygones are not bygones
There was in all of them
Yes, in all of them, a part of you.

And it was that part I loved-
Not the women in their entirety.

I wait

The bridge over the bay
Holds in its rusting iron fingers
A coldly glittering necklace
Of pearly stars. I wait.

The wind rustles in the sleepy leaves of
Trees on the shore. A night bird caws.
Writhing and rising, the fog encounters
Wet air and it goes to sleep. I wait.

The winding charts of rivers flow
into the bay. Muddy waters merge with blue
become brownish bluish yellowish.
Swirl in eddies and small currents. I wait.

The river, the bridge, the trees,
The wind, the fog and the pearly stars
All ask me, why do you wait? And I, the stranger
Tell them, I've lost my vagabond self;
It may return any time. I wait for him.

Satyapal Anand

A pout and a pouch

The pouty lip-stacked mouth is a reminder;
so are the heavy-lidded eyes showing insomnia,
her constantly present night attendant.
Both are bad for my mood, but I say,
Don't sulk. Be your normal, natural self.
Let me have the money. I *have* to make this trip.
Important for me, you see, it is.
My sister's expired and India is not another planet;
 only another country. I'll be back in a week.

The pout becomes a swollen bulge
a lump dilated by lip distension—the eyes
remain their insomniac self, no change there.
Philosopher of conjugal harmony I'm not
but life has taught me a few things, one being
don't do something that she dislikes
but if you must do it, offer her to join you.

No money, she said, for sentimental trips.
You know we are not rich, just *one* pay check
you bring, not *two*. Some do have two jobs, you know.

No money, she said and I catch the bull by its horns.
I begin a little hesitatingly . . . what if we both go?
You see, your mom is unwell also; you can see her.
Meet your other friends also, dear. I add the last punch word.

The pout gradually turns into a thin fat line;
that is natural for she is gifted with fleshy lips
so sweet to kiss: the insomniac eyes suddenly
lose their inebriated look and become alert.
Gone is her demeanor of a moment back.

Yes, she says, and the pilgrimage to the goddess shrine—
Oh, how great would that be if we go together this time!

Satyapal Anand

I rediscover my body

Never did I discover my body till my seventieth year
wrote the Hindu sage *Shankaracharya*—Now I touch
it where it aches or the dry skin cries: I am itchy.
Now it is that I've to get up often at night
and coax my urine out. Never was it like this before.

With my body I've fought a thousand battles
and won many of them. You will not think of women
I would tell my body plainly. It is a sin and unworthy
of a man of God. It would not answer but then I found
my body was not the culprit; my mind was.
You would not crave for tasty foods, I would advise it
and while it consumed simple vegetables and fruit
it never would stop craving for sweet and savory dishes.

I held my body to ransom; never did I punish my mind
for its sins of omission and commission in thought.

Now that I am three scores and ten
both my body and mind are my friends. I talk to them,
share their afflictions and woes, try to console them.
I've rediscovered my falling hair, my weakening eyesight
my falling teeth and my limbs aching. It is like
getting to know a person you have been all your life
but never cultivate friendship.

But who am I? Who is my body and who is my mind?
Are we three different entities—apart and yet akin?

The Hindu sage **Shankracharya** answers succinctly.
My body is my physical frame that I can see feel and touch;
my mind is that which controls it with its seat in my head.
I, the third apart-akin-entity remain unseen but always there.
I call it *atman*—the soul.

(A Shankracharya discourse—1980)

Satyapal Anand

I witness a killing

Watching the birdie nest in the tree has been
both a pastime and a morning hour of meditation.
In my lawn is the tree; in the tree is the nest
And I, a convalescing patient, am in my wheel chair.
A rustling newspaper is on the folding table
So is the tea kettle renewed and refurbished twice.

The birdie mom is fussing over its offspring
Chirrup . . . chirrup, it says; behave yourself when I'm gone
I'll be back with more food for all three.

Did I snooze? The baby birdies are raising a din.
What is the fuss about? I ask myself and see
a snake slithering up the branches.
Harmless it is, I know, to human beings
but a man in a wheel chair can only shout at it
and do nothing else.

The next second I see a featherless little waif
A birdie baby, snug in the snake's jaw.
The mom returns momentarily, dives at the snake
Once, twice, three times. No avail. The baby's already
swallowed up. Gone down in the bulging belly
that seems to be gorged with a few more morsels.

I stop breathing; just shout hoarsely—"Hey, wife.
Take me inside now. The sun is unbearably hot."

The Eternal Clock

Who do I ask?
When I burn up like a shooting star
And fall on the hard ground with a thud
Will someone ask, "Who was the man?"

Those who read these poems today
Will they remember me tomorrow when
I'm a just a memory and no more?
Maybe, my name lingers in their mind
like a dry flower in a book.
Maybe, some do recall a rainbow that spread
Over their horizon when they first read my poems.

Isn't it possible that some keen minds
May ask sardonically, "Who was this man
Digging potable water wells on the paths he traversed
For the thirsty ones following him?

Sheer folly is this thinking!
My better self admonishes me forcefully.
There's no truck between fame and renown.
Fame is but a matter of a second on the fame clock
Till the last sand grain falls.

Satyapal Anand

Mother-of-Pearl Shells

Shells—mothers-to-be
Of pearls—bright, beamy, brilliant
Untouched, chaste and pure
Mothers-to-be, virginal shells
Mary-like, scattered all over on the sand
Soaking sun and wind
Heaving, turning over . . .
Waiting!

Waiting!
Heaving, turning over
Seamless apertures half open
Awaiting, anticipating
Expecting love and affection
A vagabond cloud sends to the sand and soil
His pearly drops of rain.
Shells—expectant mothers of pearls
Eagerly await their impregnation.

Await their impregnation.
A pearly drop of benediction
From above and beyond and unseen
But palpably here and now
Might just find the inviting aperture
Enter like a bright sun ray
A bud-like inner flowering
Of the famed pearl of Nazareth.

The famed pearl of Nazareth.
Untouched, chaste and pure
Mothers-to-be, virginal shells
Mary-like, scattered all over on the sand
Soaking sun and wind
Heaving, turning over . . .
Waiting!

The Insouciant I

The sky, wearing one glittering eye-glass
Looks accusingly at me—where's your honor?
It asks. Shameful it was for you to deny her the
opportunity . . .

Opportunity to seduce me? I ask.
Seventyish she is—a widow of eighteen years
trying to engulf me in her upper and lower
chasms? Both deep and vacuumed clean?
No substance there, Sir-G, a hollow head
and a vacuous womb. No! Sir-G, No!

The glittering eye-glass slides down to the nose-tip
So what? The sky asks: Is your male ego well-fed now?
Forsaken by her dreams she lies sick now.
In trying to fill her vacuolated head with knowledge
she has had a thousand reveries of affairs . . .

I cut the single-lens-sky-eye short—What about
her lower drawer? Has it become solvent again?
That was full of holes too—a vacuolated container.
I don't know, the somber sky said, I never could
Look that far down; you know my monocle
would have fallen . . . He was about to say *inside*
but he checked himself in time.

I said, "Next time, O high priest of Heavens
when you look down, tie it to your bushy eyebrow
so it wouldn't fall. So far as I'm concerned,
I am unconcerned. You see, Sir G, I lack grace.

Like Donne's legendary lovers, I die
a hundred times in one affair, but when I rise again,
I am still a petty, parochial Satyapal*
So insouciant I am.

*The name in Sanskrit means "The Truth Keeper".

A Freudian, a Jungian, a Schopenhauerian and I

The three were there and so was I.
Look at this mental case, F said about me
He is a ravished ruin and in his debris we have to
Discover the man he used to be. J said, I agree.
S said, he has been polite to others all through
I believe; politeness is to human nature what
heat is to wax. In short, he has melted.

F said, to me it is a simple case of sex repressed.
He never articulated it. You see, like hatred
sex must be articulated or, like hatred, it will
produce an internal malaise.

J said, in part, I believe you are right, F, but
a little off the mark. Every malaise is not sex repressed;
some can be sex expressed also. Just look at him.
To me, he seems a classical case of over-indulgence
Not only in sex, but all joy-able and enjoy-able pursuits.

I don't agree, S said morosely
I don't agree either, F said sardonically
I do agree, suddenly I found my tongue.

POEMS ORIGINALLY

WRITTEN IN URDU

Crime and Punishment

Originally written in Urdu   جرم و سزا

Once on every moonlit night
He visited me—the angel
The reckoning auditor of all my deeds he was.
From him I would get to know the latest
what I had done to earn bad or good points
and how my balance stood at the moment.

Last night he came again
Was a little thoughtful with pity writ large
On his angelic face.
I never could think, he said,
That your poetry might earn you bad points . . .
Well, it has.

Aghast I was. But before I could speak
He said, "Rare are people who speak or write
We never take speech or writing as a deed.
You, it seems, have earned both good and bad points.
And the reckoned balance is rather lopsided."

Does it weigh on the bad side? I asked.
He read something jotted down on the palm of his hand
(I couldn't see): it shimmered like a cell phone.
Finally, he said, "Well, it seems it is even."

So, I asked him, what do I do?
He smiled (Do angels ever smile? I didn't know)
And simply said: "Keep on writing whatever you want.
We'll balance it at the end of your life, my man."

I wanted to ask him something about poetizing heresy.
Without looking back, he spoke from the void
No hurry. Wait for the next month
    O ill-versed good poet!

(1962)

Incomplete Characters

Originally written in Urdu.   ادھورے کردار

How indeed would all tales
Of beauty and love ever reach a summation?
The characters in these stories
Were incomplete, we all know.

The goddess of beauty
Had her hands severed
And the god of love
Was but a blind brat!

(1958)

Flint

Originally written in Urdu ... چقماق

The first snowfall of winter
The northern most town in Canada
She, a Phoenician Astarte
And I a war lord from India
Conjoined by a kind fate of a fast moment
Now to be separated by a cruel kismet.

Blue were the eyes, bluer still
Was the depth in them, abysmal, unfathomable.
Looking deep into the still mercurial sheen
Was an experience—and I knew it.

I held her hand in mine.
Was she seeking some warmth? I didn't know
But her breath coming in a vaporous heat
Could enkindle the long-lost fire
I had no means of knowing it.

Days that expired in buoyant flames
Had been left far behind
Their ash was buried all these years
But I knew that her deep blue eyes
Had the flint that could enkindle it afresh.
I had only to look into the two mercury pools
Deep, long and lovingly.

Satyapal Anand

The Difficult Path

Originally written in Urdu . . . . راہ پر خار

Turning, twisting, troublesome is the path
I have been walking on—and then
Suddenly there is fork; the path divides into two.
I can look far ahead on one
But only a few yards ahead on the other.
Uneven, rough and bumpy is one
Rugged and craggy—it is all the way I can see.
Smooth and level is the other path
Flat, stable and symmetrical
A few yards that I can see are inviting.
Both paths vie with each other to attract me
one inviting, the other plainly uninviting.

The second one welcomes me in a velvety tone:
Oh, poor old man, it seems to say
Look at your torn, thorn-studded soles
Walked all your life you have, I know
Struggling each yard of the way
Straining and striving
Stress and strain have been your lot in life.
Come and walk on my soft bosom
A few yards it is and then . . .
You'll be beyond trouble for eternity.

The first one says, tired you are, I know
Don't come unless you must. I go a long way
Thorny and troublesome I am
Cluttered with disease and debility that

All old men experience in waning years.
Courage is the only *mantra* you have to chant.
With me you'll live straining and striving
but live you will; what do you say?
Is there a hurry to die? No, none!

Wanderer, trekker I have been all my life
I tell myself; jaunts and junkets are pilgrimages
For me, move on this path I will.
Toil is travel, I know, no rest for me
None needed, none ordained.

(2005)

The Cuckold's Anthem

Originally written in Urdu . . . زن مرید کا قومی ترانہ

A goddess thou art
And I a mere worshipper, adoring and adulating
O goddess divine, heaven-bestowed benediction
For me thou art.
A mere nothing I am, or something, if at all,
A slave, a happy and contented slave, only yours!

Happy I am as a dreg
A scrap of self that once husbanded
A headstrong mare
Riding over mounds and dugouts with agile dexterity.
Now? No longer that gifted I am, you know.

I crave, even now, my long last role
Ache and yearn for the lost empire
A king sans crown, a husband sans husbandry
I know, who I am, but you O queen
I serve and feel good.
Give good gratification, once in a while,
To the willing slave that I am.

(1992)

The soul mate she chose

Originally written in Urdu: با نسے اک معصوم عورت کا مقدر

Green and fresh like a blade of grass
Holding a dew drop on its bosom
She could have danced in the breeze—but
The lively, frolicsome girl
Had chosen a soul mate
Staid and grave, a living corpse
One, who could never turn back to life.

A pearl-sewn headscarf of
Seven colors of the rainbow
Green and yellow laces adorning her neck
Bouncing and bounding, flitting and fluttering
A cute bird, she could enjoy her Life – but
The tree on which she had made a nest
Was dry and seer, a leafless column of wood
One, who could never give her shelter.

A sweet, euphonious note she was
Melodious and mellifluent,
Lilting and lyrical
Difficult it was to merge into a symphony
But when she did, she was the sweetest note of all.
Honey dew she brought to the listeners with her voice

Satyapal Anand

But the *sitar* player she had chosen didn't have strength in his fingers to enliven her.

Pity her for the soul-mate she chose!

(1999)

The Biblical Age

Originally written in Urdu . . . انجیل میں لکھی عمر

    Colors-all confused, deranged and disturbed
Sounds-all inaudible, spent and sparse
Mist and fog, haze and steam
Nothing is bright and sunny and clear!

    What is this state of mind? What kind, indeed?
Is it a beckoning bivouac or the final destination
That I espy in the near distance?
Are my steps advancing or retreating?
Where could they retreat?
To the threshold on which I had buried
Once upon a time
Both my sight and my hearing
And had then thought I would never be back?
For having lost myself do I go in search of
A new *persona* beyond the horizon?

    Seven soft-paced decades have walked by
I never heard their footsteps—and now
Having crossed yet another decade
Don't I feel I have cheated the biblical age norm?
And continue to cheat it every new morn?

                 (2001)

            Satyapal Anand

Ululate, my utopian tongue

Originally written in Urdu. انقلاب زنده باد

Once it was, once only
   when I was just sixteen
   ululating my utopian tongue
   I had raised a slogan
   Inqualab Zinda-baad
   "Long live revolution."

The British rule in India
   my motherland, I hated.
   Revolution was the way
   to do it, I was told.
   A policeman came running
   hit me on the head.
   Take your revolution, he said
   here, here and here.
   Three baton strokes
   On my head and shoulders
   made stars swirl round my head.

Today is ten years later.
   My motherland is free.
   So are all policemen
   who run amok and hit
   all who cry revolution,
   thrice, thrice and thrice
   nine times in all.

Ululate, my utopian tongue.
  Keep on ululating
  till you are tired
  or cut out by a policeman
  with a knife.

(1957)

A Stranger in his home

Originally written in Urdu گھر میں اجنبی

Not been able to laugh
For years, I smiled and laughed
Once only in the sanctity of my own rook
And suddenly they were all there
My wife and children
Peering from behind the half-shut door.

Thought probably—all of them
With no exception, that their old man
Had gone crazy. Why should he laugh?
Why, indeed? On an ordinary day,
Without a proper cause for jubilation?

Had I, in my depression and melancholy
Heaved a long, audible sigh,
Cried out in anguish
They wouldn't have been surprised.
I knew.

(1960)

Live blistering coals

Originally written in Urdu شرار لفظ

Cry you might
All you can—the whole night
O my love
Yet you can't douche them.
My poems are but
Blistering coals—
Held in paper's fists.

(1954)

A Precautionary Measure

Originally written in Urdu حفظ ماتقدم

    I always do that, I told the doctor
No reason why it should cause palpitation
You see, before I go to sleep
I clasp my hands right over my heart
Tighten them up-lest . . .

    Yes, lest? The doctor asked.

    Well, I don't know, I said
But I always think that I would save myself
From flying away in my sleep.

(1959)

✳

Hurrying Toward Collapse

Urdu title قیامت ِ صغرا دور نہیں ہے

Alligator shoes, name brand socks
but hairy tibias beneath
Sharkskin suits from London's men's store
Goggles with a price tag of two hundred dollars
Trimmed moustaches, dyed hair—a Lenin-like beard
Intellectually-oriented, but essential in his appearance
The Prime Minister of a penny-wise nation
With an army that consumes half of its budget
Comes for a United Nations meeting in New York.

A five star hotel's wing for sixty of his staff
Costs fifty thousand a day or an hour, no one knows
But what everyone knows is what's happening back home.
His people are dying in droves—with hunger
And floods and gunning down of innocent
Men, women and children in the name of God.
Girls' schools are blown up for—they say—
Female literacy is a curse according to the Imam
Babies are denied polio vaccination for the
Oral drops that sheath them from the disease is –
They say – Satan's brew of sin.

God forbid, نعوذ بالله
But it does seem the land of my forefathers is
Hurrying toward collapse.

Satyapal Anand

Winter-I

Urdu title ··· زمستاں

Canada

The house speaks. It is a cold rasping voice
not unheard before. Its pleura and throat chords
are pneumatically effected. Get out in the snow.
It orders me without a preamble.

Outside a frozen evening warns me. Go back, it
says. The house is not freezing but I am.
I disregard the evening's advice and stay.
I get busy watching a row of snowmen that
stand like white sentries all along the street
All in the front yards of houses that are lit.
Carrots as noses they all have and I – don't know
what they have for eyes.
Their headgears have blown away, but they stand.
At attention like soldiers, they are alert, *qui vive.*

I walk down the street, muffler and wool cap up
hands down in my pockets, gloves I hate. I walk
an ordinary, unremarkable, elderly man going,
not on an errand, but simply to test his pacing prowess.
Suddenly the edges of light harden in one house.
I stop. There are voices, irate and angry inside.
My stopping is noticed; the voices cease. I proceed.

My house probably feels lonely without me.
Only I can hear its call.
"Flurries have started again," it says. "You old fool,
come back. Hurry up and raise the temperature
by one more degree.
I am freezing, don't you see?"

Winter-II

Urdu title موسم سرما

India

Keekar trees don't make a sound in the wind.
Their leaves and thorns both are spike-like
An inch to two inches ling, thorns can puncture your feet
Or even deflate cycle tires.

Winters in India are like *Keekar trees*—but
the one in ninety-one was biting and blistery.
Piercing winds blew-and with no electric heating,
we just sat around an open hearth of live coals.
Men read, women knitted and children played.
Tired of sitting in a chair or cross-legged on a durree,
One could always go back to the cozy bed.

That winter was not much different from others
except that I got married and stayed put inside
the nuptial room most of the time
—except, of course, when I went to work.

A sage has said only patience can survive the winter.
I prayed that I have patience in bushels
so the winter stays and spring doesn't come.
In summer with no electric fan
All family members – the groom and the bride being no exception
slept on the top roof under an open sky—and visible
to all prying eyes.